Hug the pocket to find my book dedicated to
Carol, Cathy, Susie & Laurie

Copyright 2021 by Barbara Menzel

What's in the Pocket?

Story by Barbara Menzel

Art by Andy Menzel

Do you have a pocket?
What could be in a pocket?
Let's look.

Can you find your pocket?
What's in the pocket?

Roll your hand across the pocket.
Honk the horn.

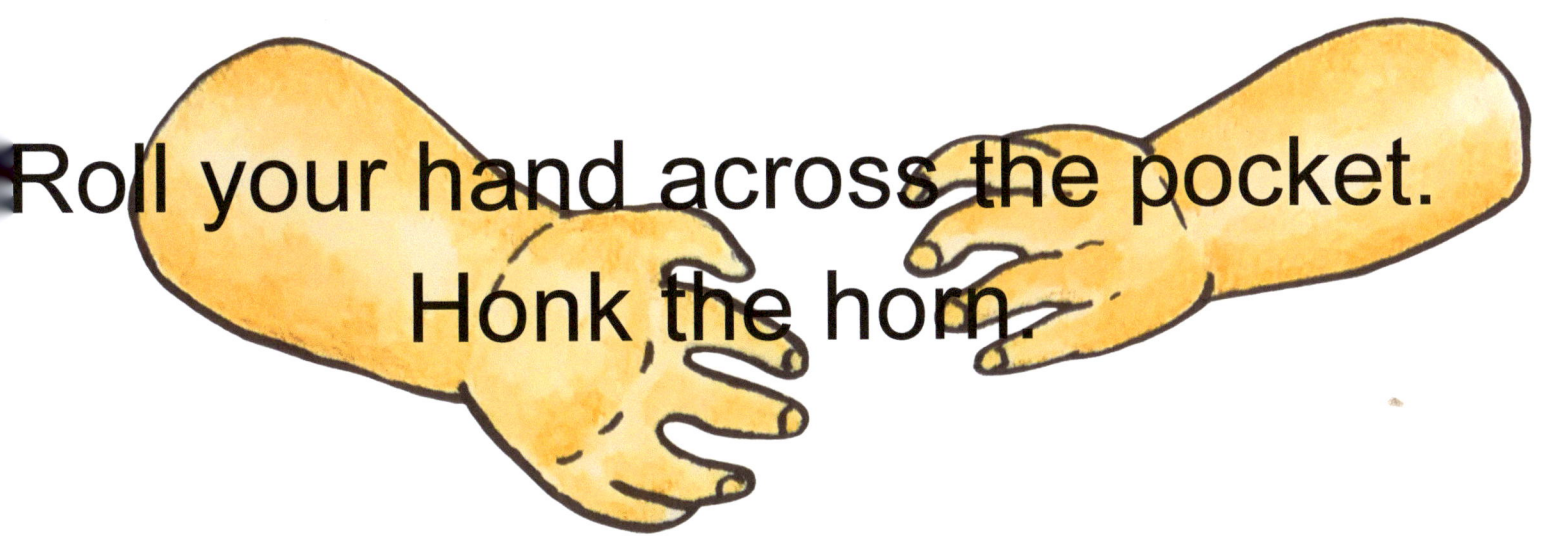

Beep. Beep. Vroom. Vroom.
What's in the pocket?

A car.

Throw out sparkles.
It's a treasure.

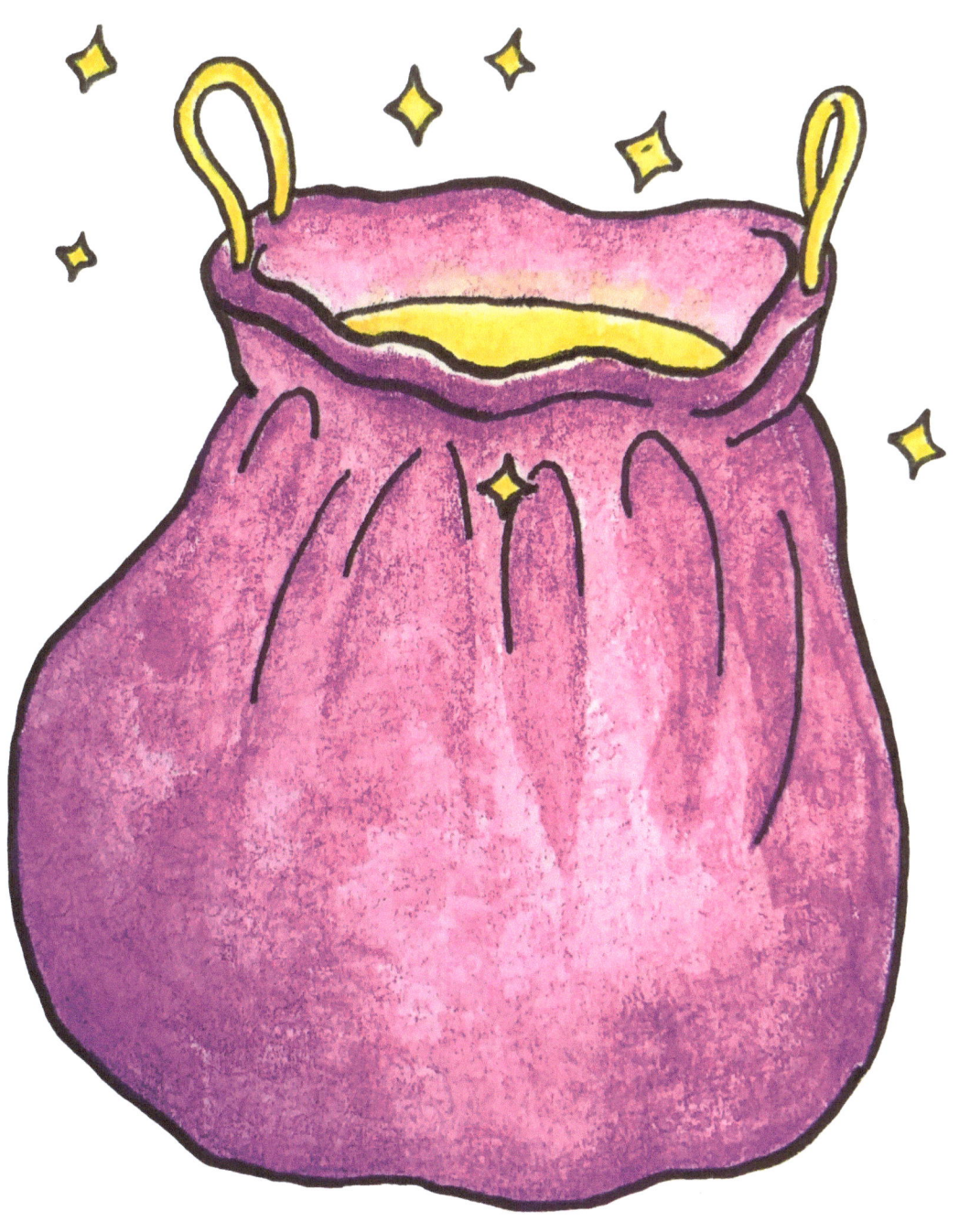

What's in the pocket?

Shiny gems.

Pick it up.
Clean the pocket.
Remove the dirt.
What's in the pocket?

A rock.

Tickle the pocket.
Laugh out loud.
Ha! Ha! Ha!
What's in the pocket?

A feather.

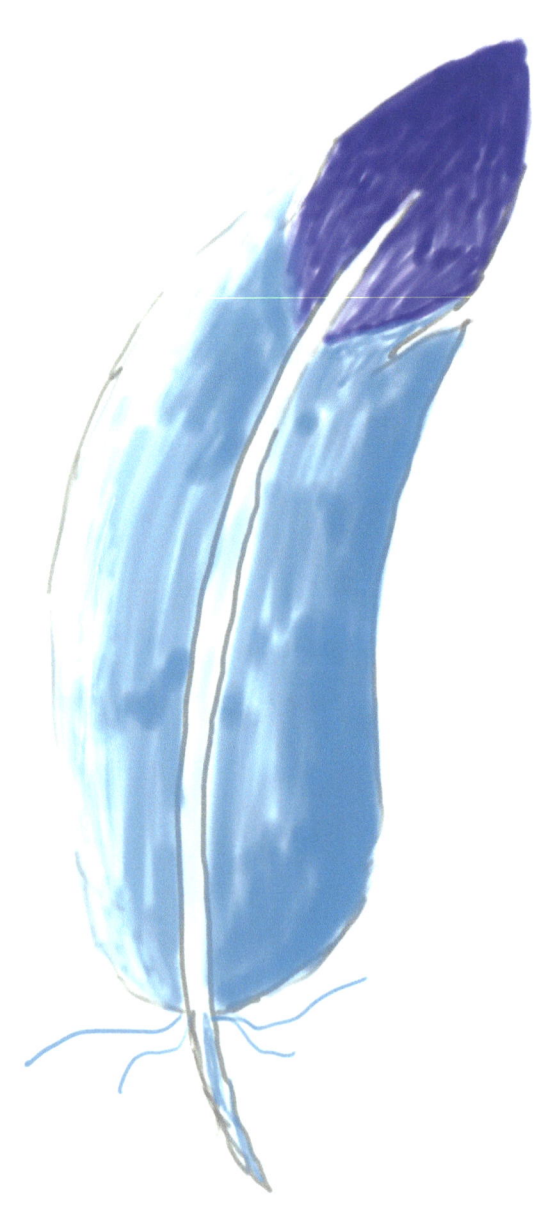

Move slowly across the pocket.
Look up to the sky.
It shines bright.
What's in the pocket?

A star.

Move your hand back and forth.
See the magic appear.
Color the world.
What's in the pocket?

Three crayons.

Shake the pocket.
I hear a sound.
Jingle. Jingle.
What's in the pocket?

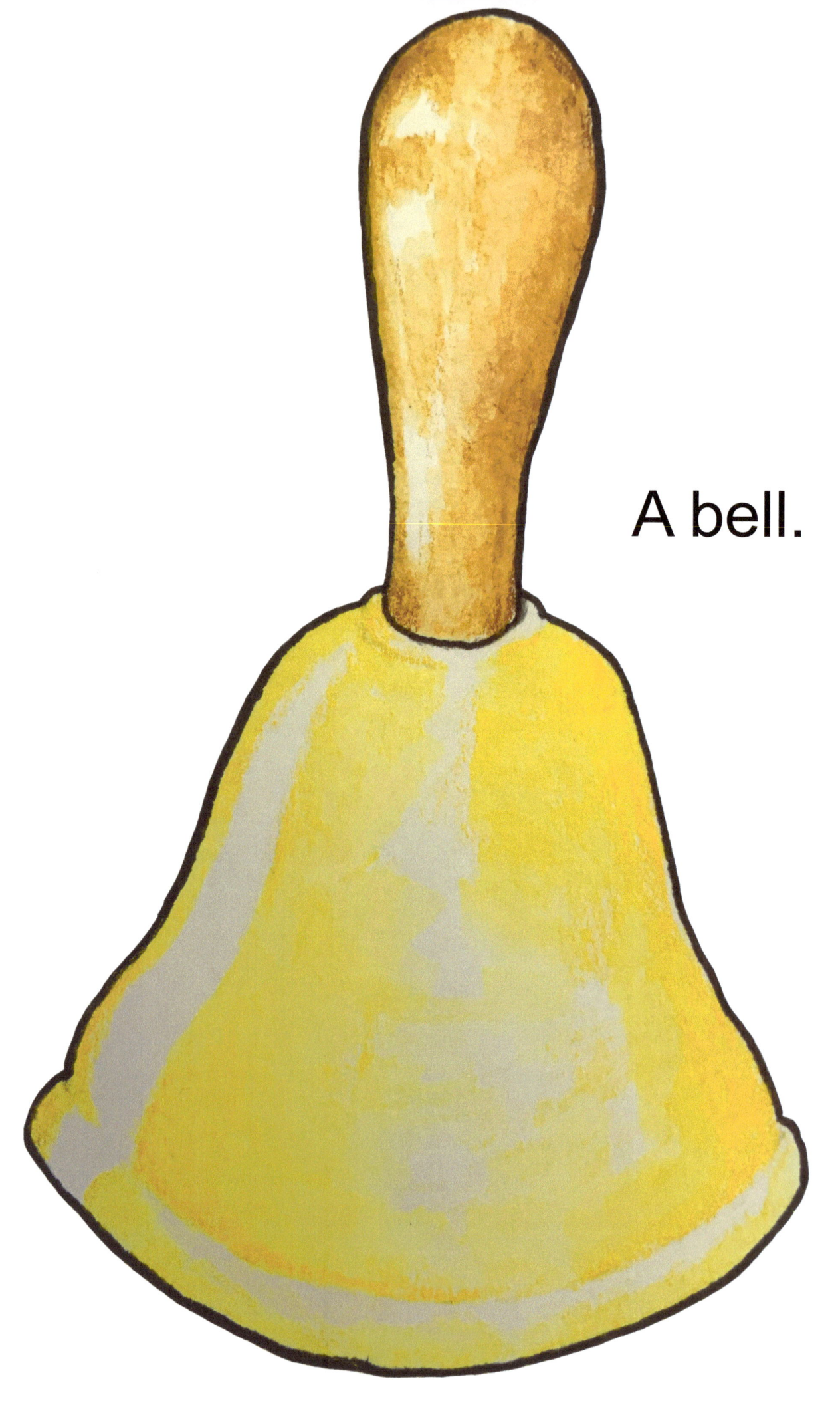

A bell.

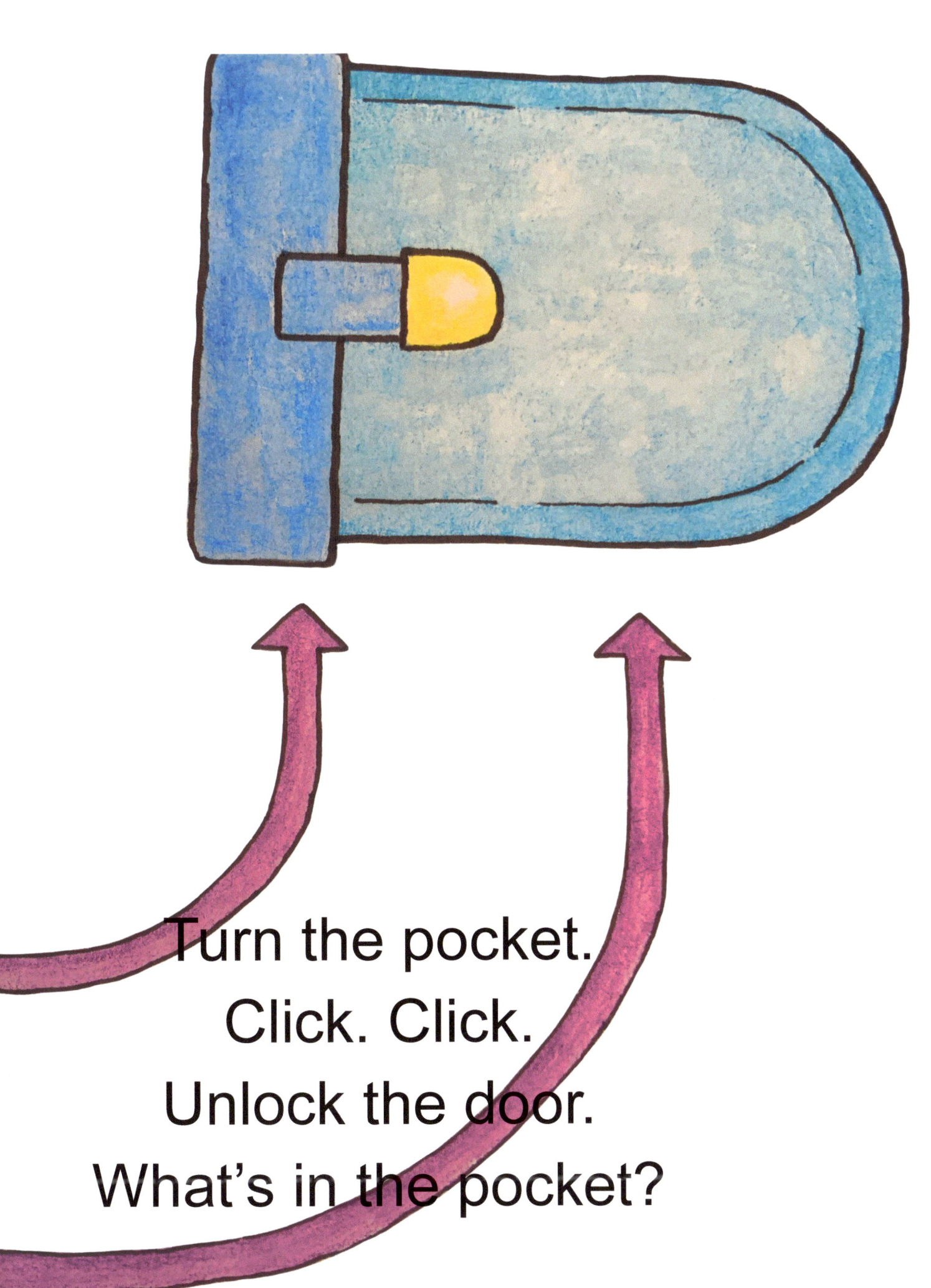

Turn the pocket.
Click. Click.
Unlock the door.
What's in the pocket?

A key.

Gently touch the pocket.
Give it love.
Hug the pocket.
What's in the pocket?

A heart.

Wave your hand above the pocket.
Rock back and forth.
Don't get splashed.

What's in the pocket?

A boat.

Fly by the pocket.
Move your wings up and down.

Flutter through the air.

What's in the pocket?

A butterfly.

Squeeze it tight.
Look for the piggy bank.
Toss it in and watch it grow.
What's in the pocket?

A penny.

Look at all the things that were in the pockets.

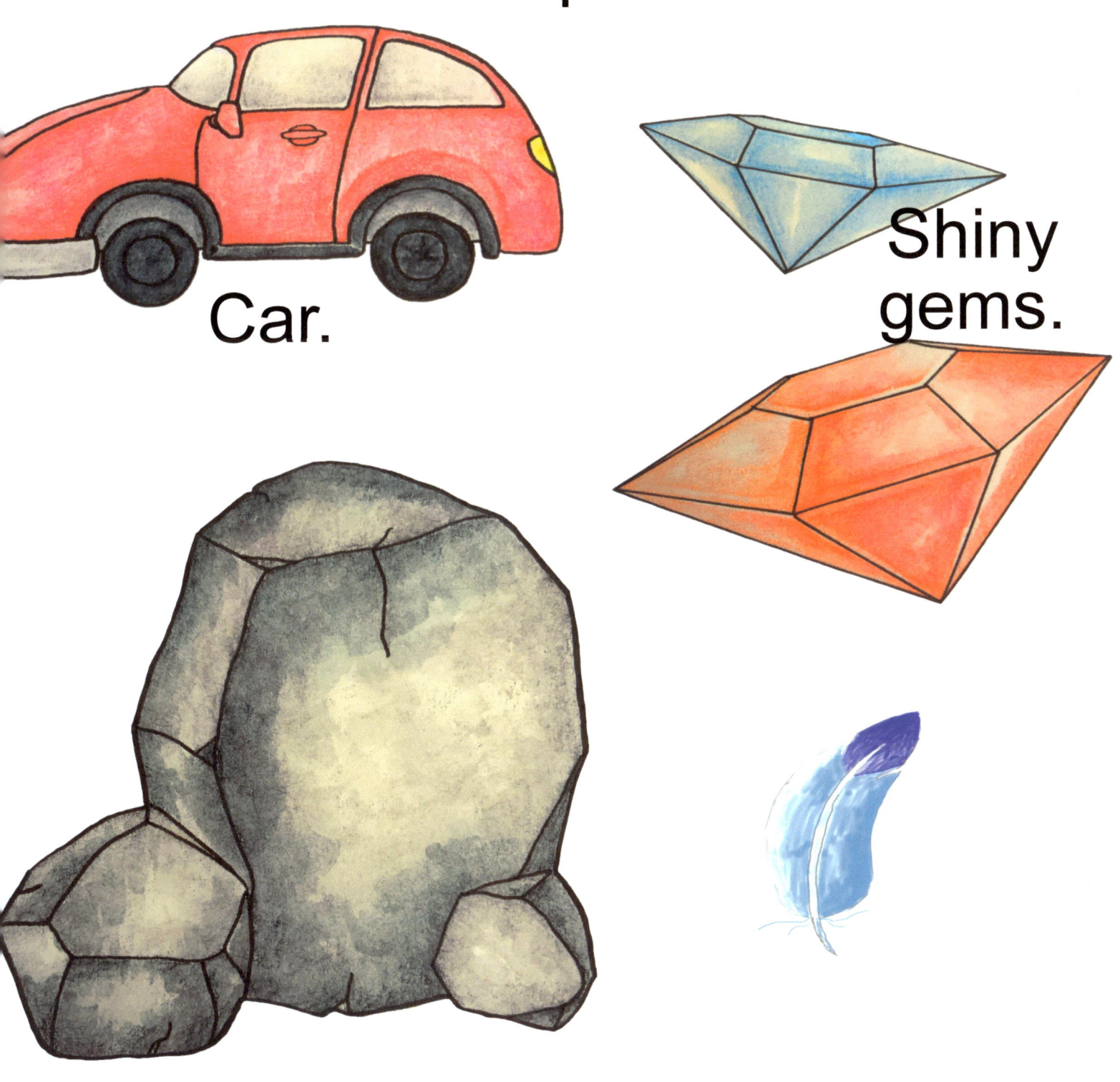

Car.

Shiny gems.

Rock.

Feather.

Bell.

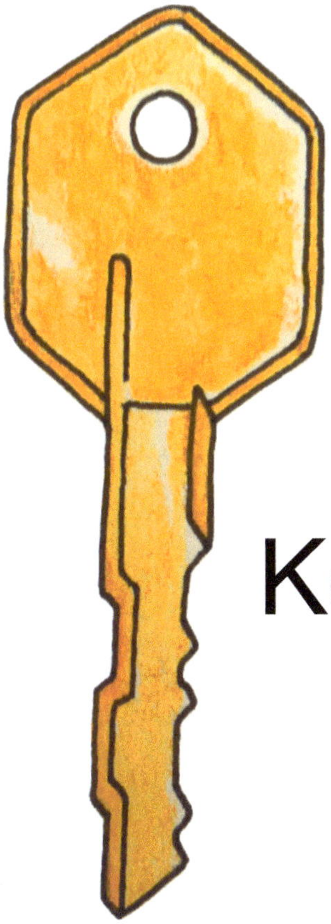

Key.

Butterfly.

Penny.

Do you have a pocket?
Can you find your pocket?

What's in the pocket?

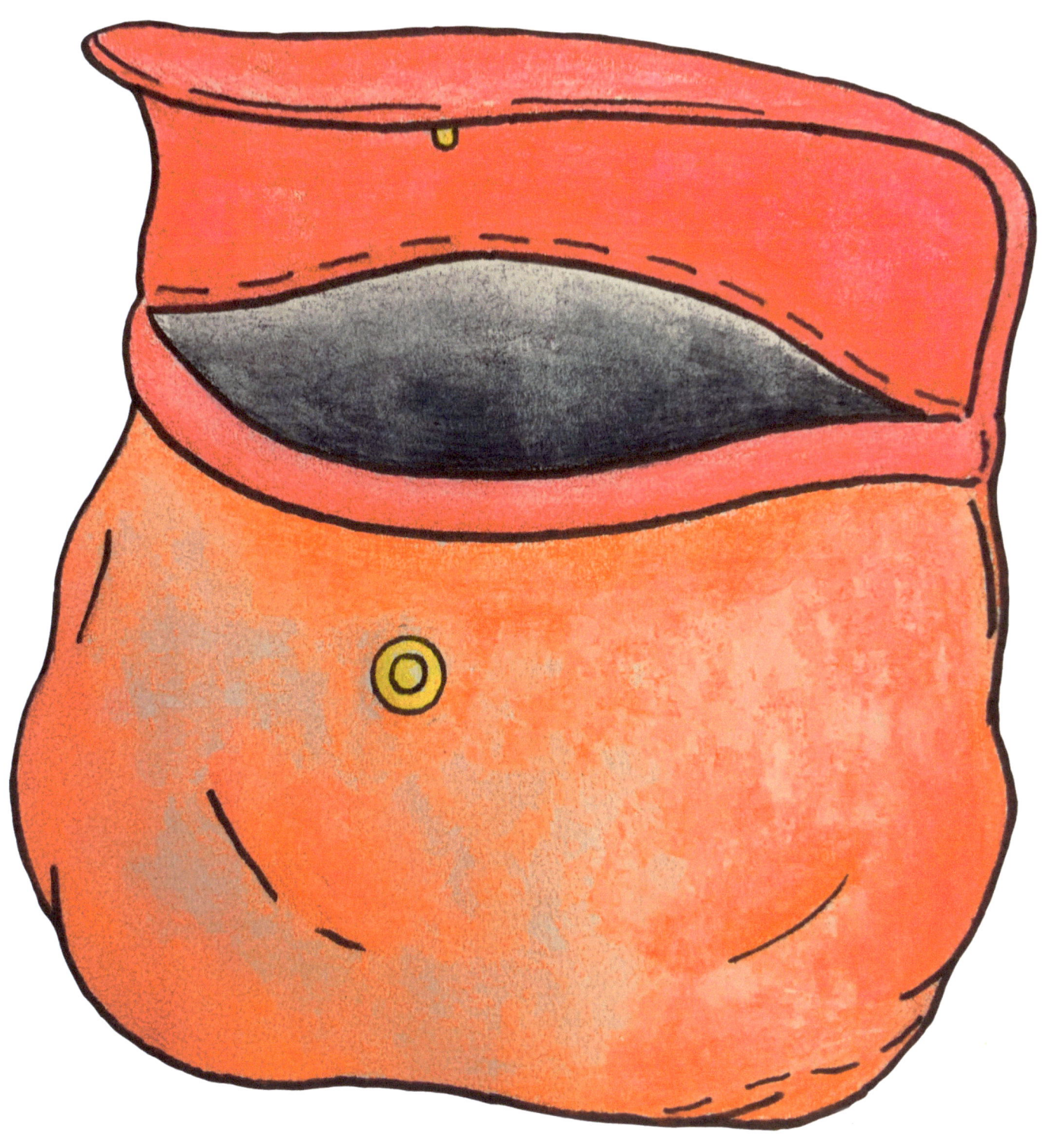

www.ingramcontent.com/pod-product-compliance
Lightning Source LLC
Chambersburg PA
CBHW041715160426
43209CB00018B/1846